Minibeasts

also edited by Robert Fisher

AMAZING MONSTERS
Verses to Thrill and Chill

GHOSTS GALORE
Haunting Verse

FUNNY FOLK
Poems about People

WITCH WORDS
Poems of Magic and Mystery

PET POEMS

MINIBEASTS

Poems about Little Creatures

Edited by
Robert Fisher

Illustrated by
Kay Widdowson

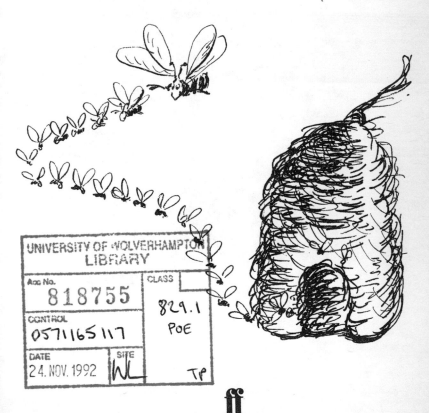

ff
faber and faber
LONDON · BOSTON

First published in 1992
by Faber and Faber Limited
3 Queen Square London WC1N 3AU

Photoset by Wilmaset Ltd, Birkenhead, Wirral
Printed in Great Britain by Clays Ltd, St Ives plc

A CIP record for this book is available from the British Library.

ISBN 0–571–16511–7

Contents

Morning, noon and night-time too
In every garden you will find
Near at hand or far-off hiding
Insect armies multiplying
Bugs of every shape and size
Eating, sleeping, living, dying
A dragon world of tiny things
Scuttling, crawling, hopping, flying
Turn these leaves and you can see
Secret creatures – minibeasts!

Robert Fisher

There be four things which are little upon the earth
But they are exceeding wise;
The ants are a people not strong,
Yet they prepare their meat in the summer;
The conies are but a feeble folk,
Yet they make their houses in the rocks;
The locusts have no king,
Yet go they forth all of them by bands;
The spider taketh hold with her hands,
And is in kings' palaces.

                                    The Book of Proverbs

Black is his colour
And he comes out of darkness
To a space of light
Where the grass rattles
And the wind booms.

In his home underground
The stones are silent
Roots and seeds make no noise.

Like fine wires
His legs tremble
Over the ground.
Raindrops hiss and explode
Around him
But he runs zig-zagging
From their cold touch.

At last one raindrop,
Bright balloon of water,
Bursts on his back
Becoming his own flood.
Frantic, he spins,
Finds ground again, and scurries
Towards some crack in an enormous Ark.

Zoë Bailey

Ants, although Admirable,
Are Awfully Aggravating

The busy ant works hard all day
And never stops to rest or play.
He carries things ten times his size,
And never grumbles, whines or cries.
And even climbing flower stalks,
He always runs, he never walks.
He loves his work, he never tires,
And never puffs, pants or perspires.

Yet though I praise his boundless vim
I am not really fond of him.

Walter R. Brooks

I buzz, I buzz, I buzz
because I am a Bee,
I never rest
in my own nest
except when I've
filled up a hive
with *excelicious* Honey.
From West Ealing
to Darjeeling
no other creature can
produce one jot
or tiny spot
of my divine confection:
no, not for love
or health or wealth
no, sir, not even for money
can any factory
make satisfactory
natural Norfolk honey.
From this you see
that I, the Bee,
by natural selection
am cleverer than
machines or man
and very near perfection.

George Barker

Bees

Down in the valley
and up on the mountain high
in nature's endless glory
they seek their prey.
But when they have sipped
from a hundred flowers
and made their honey,
for whom is their labour,
for whom their nectar?

Lo Yin

Bee! I'm expecting you!
Was saying Yesterday
To Somebody you know
That you were due –

The Frogs got Home last Week –
Are settled, and at work –
Birds, mostly back –
The Clover warm and thick –

You'll get my Letter by
The seventeenth; Reply
Or better, be with me –
Yours, Fly.

Emily Dickinson

Poring on Caesar's death with earnest eye,
I heard a fretful buzzing in the pane:
'Poor bee!' I cried, 'I'll help thee by and by,'
Then dropp'd mine eyes upon the page again.
Alas! I did not rise; I help'd him not:
In the great voice of Roman history
I lost the pleading of the window bee,
And all his woes and troubles were forgot.
In pity for the mighty chief who bled
Beside his rival's statue, I delay'd
To serve the little insect's present need,
And so he died for lack of human aid.

I could not change the Roman's destiny:
I might have set the honey-maker free.

Charles Tennyson Turner

Xestobium nifovillosum
bangs his head
on the floor of his burrow.
The superstitious hearer
thinks death is coming.
In the quiet of the night
as you watch by the dying
you hear the ticking of
the death watch beetle.

Michael Harrison

Xylocorus Galactinus

Xylocorus galactinus
is a predator.
His closest relation
lives in our warm beds
but he crawls through
manure-heaps and
other odorously steaming places.
His friends call him
the hot-bed bug.

Michael Harrison

The Bookworm

A moth munching words. How weird!
a worm swallowing man's sayings,
a sneak-thief feasting in the dark
on a poet's fine songs.
And the stealer none the wiser
for the words he has swallowed.

Old English Riddle

How soft the sound
of butterflies
eating!

Kyoshi

At the butterflies
the caged bird gazes sadly –
just look at its eyes!

Issa

Garden butterfly
as the baby crawls, it flies
she crawls, it flies

Issa

A falling flower
is returning to its branch –
Ah, a butterfly!

Arakida Moritake

Flat on my back
beneath the freckling sun,
three butterflies sail around me,
and very gently, one
settles on my burning face,
folding his dusty wings,
as if he liked the place;
and one hovers a little while
before he decides to land
with cool and delicate feet
upon the thumb of my right hand,
but soon changes his mind, and does not stay
to keep me company, skimming soundlessly away
into the flowers and trees:
and one goes on flitting around
my head at perfect ease,
and will not be my guest.

But how glad I am
that two of them made me
their resting place a minute or so,
believing I was a flower or tree.

Leonard Clark

Blossoms fall like snowflakes
on cool, deep, dark-green moss,
they lie white-heaped in scented drifts
before the courtyard gates.

Butterflies, not knowing
the days of spring are done
still chase floating petals
across a garden wall.

Chu Miao Tuan

Flying Crooked

The butterfly, a cabbage-white,
(His honest idiocy of flight)
Will never now, it is too late,
Master the art of flying straight,
Yet has – who knows so well as I? –
A just sense of how not to fly:
He lurches here and here by guess
And God and hope and hopelessness.
Even the aerobatic swift
Has not his flying-crooked gift.

Robert Graves

I look like a flower you could pick. My delicate wings
Flutter over the cabbages. I don't make
Any noise ever. I'm among silent things.
    Also I easily break.

I have seen the nets in your hands. At first I thought
A cloud had come down but then I noticed you
With your large pink hand and arm. I was nearly caught
    But fortunately I flew

Away in time, hid while you searched, then took
To the sky, was out of your reach. Like a nameless flower
I tried to appear. Can't you be happy to look?
    Must you possess with your power?

Elizabeth Jennings

I was round and small like a pearl,
Then long and slender, as brave as an earl.
Since like a hermit I lived in a cell,
And now like a rogue in the wide world I dwell.

Anonymous

The Caterpillar

Brown and furry
Caterpillar in a hurry;
Take your walk
To the shady leaf or stalk.

May no toad spy you,
May the little birds pass by you;
Spin and die,
To live again a butterfly.

Christina Rossetti

These morning airs
See them blowing
Caterpillar hairs!

Buson

The Tickle Rhyme

'Who's that tickling my back?' said the wall.
'Me,' said a small
caterpillar. 'I'm learning
to crawl.'

Ian Serraillier

'Little Arabella Miller'

Little Arabella Miller
Found a woolly caterpillar,
First it crawled upon her mother
Then upon her baby brother.
All said 'Arabella Miller,
Take away that caterpillar!'

Anonymous

With innumerable little footsteps
I go through life
but, Lord,
I can never
get to the end of myself!
It's a queer sensation
to be a multitude
that follows itself
in Indian file!
True,
it's the first step that counts
or, rather,
the first foot.
All that matters
is to be in step
with one's self:
I only ask,
Lord,
to jog along
one in spirit
without troublesome
reticences.

Amen.

Carmen Bernos de Gasztold
translated by Rumer Godden

The centipede was happy quite
until the toad in fun
said, 'Pray which leg comes after which?'
This wrought her mind to such a pitch
she lay distracted in a ditch
considering how to run.

Anonymous

Of all the strange creatures that live in your house,
Stranger than any flea, beetle or mouse,
I am the strangest you ever won't find.
Wherever I travel, I leave holes behind.

Whole-holes and half-holes and three-quarter-holes,
I leave them in trousers and socks and shoe soles,
Slippers and jumpers and pockets and sheets,
And tights and tea-towels and cane-bottomed seats.

I leave holes in curtains and elbows of jackets,
I also snap strings in your old tennis raquets.
Each place that I go I leave you a hole,
And . . .

 olé.

Ian Larmont

The cricket, like a knuckled rubber-band,
Whirrs from the launching platform of my hand
Without much notion where he's going to land.

But does he mind the jump or the surprise?
Suppose we chanced to be each other's size?
I know I wouldn't stay. I'd close my eyes.

And jump. Are bodies chosen with a pin?
My own seems suitable for being in,
But why pale pink, rather than pale green skin?

And does some giant, wishing me no harm,
Peruse me, perfect, on his unseen palm?
What creatures stir upon the cricket's arm?

The worlds are gears upon the wheels of chance.
The worlds retreat and worlds in worlds advance.
The creatures dance. And lead themselves a dance.

Leaping the grasses like a leafy lancer,
The cricket does not know that he's a dancer.
I ask the questions, but he *is* the answer

And all the summer's day he needn't think
But simply jump, a jointed tiddlewink,
A perfect alpha minus in green ink.

John Fuller

Far off mountain peaks
are reflected in its eyes
– the dragonfly!

Issa

See the dragonfly
his face is practically nothing
– but an eye!

Chisoku

A Dragonfly

When the heat of the summer
Made drowsy the land,
A dragonfly came
And sat on my hand.

With its blue jointed body,
And wings like spun glass,
It lit on my fingers
As though they were grass.

Eleanor Farjeon

Today I saw the dragon-fly
Come from the wells where he did lie.

An inner impulse rent the veil
Of his old husk: from head to tail
Came out clear plates of sapphire mail.

He dried his wings: like gauze they grew;
Through crofts and pastures wet with dew
A living flash of light he flew.

Alfred, Lord Tennyson

They used to fear
That while asleep
Into the ear
This beast would creep;
Through waxy passages
Would tread
To penetrate
The very head,
Until at last
It would attain
The grey and wrinkled
Human brain
Where, after pausing
For the view,
It probably
Would start to chew . . .

Believe this,
You must be a dope.
It's just
An old wives' tale.

I hope.

Eric Finney

The tiny fish enjoy themselves
in the sea.
Quick little splinters of life,
their little lives are fun to them
in the sea.

                        D. H. Lawrence

'*Swarms of minnows show their little heads*'

Swarms of minnows show their little heads,
Staying their wavy bodies 'gainst the streams
To taste the luxury of sunny beams
Tempered with coolness. How they ever wrestle
With their own sweet delight, and ever nestle
With their silver bellies on the pebbly sand.
If you but scantily hold out the hand,
That very instant not one will remain;
But turn your eye, and they are there again.

                        John Keats

Great fleas have little fleas upon their backs to bite 'em,
And little fleas have lesser fleas and so on ad infinitum.
And the great fleas themselves in turn have greater fleas to
  go on,
While these again have greater still and greater still, and so
  on.

Mary Augusta de Morgan

For the fleas also
night must be so very long
and very lonely

Issa

'A flea and a fly in a flue'

A flea and a fly in a flue
Were caught, so what could they do?
Said the fly, 'Let us flee.'
'Let us fly,' said the flea.
So they flew through a flow in the flue.

Anonymous

Adam
Had 'em

Anonymous

The Fly

Little Fly,
Thy summer's play
My thoughtless hand
Has brush'd away.

Am not I
A fly like thee?
Or art not thou
A man like me?

For I dance,
And drink, and sing,
Till some blind hand
Shall brush my wing.

William Blake

How large unto the tiny fly
    Must little things appear! –
A rosebud like a feather bed,
    Its prickle like a spear;

A dewdrop like a looking-glass,
    A hair like golden wire;
The smallest grain of mustard-seed
    As fierce as coals of fire;

A loaf of bread, a lofty hill;
    A wasp, a cruel leopard;
And specks of salt as bright to see
    As lambkins to a shepherd.

                    Walter de la Mare

'A diner while dining at Crewe'

A diner while dining at Crewe,
Found a rather large fly in his stew,
Said the waiter, 'Don't shout
And wave it about
Or the rest will be wanting one too!'

                    Anonymous

Each autumn in the kitchen
A fly remains. The same?
How can we tell? Except
It seems to grow more tame.

If you're a house-fly
Then I wonder why
You bang on the glass
That keeps you from grass.

You know by my flapping hand I hate your flight;
So why do you want to kiss me in the night?

Fly, who's been very naughty on my dough-
Nut, why do I push the window, let you go?

Fly in the milk, I spoon you out alive
And grieve you're too bedraggled to survive.

Still fly against the wall – it is as if
I stood asleep upon an upright cliff.

A fly on the kitchen pane –
Surely that fly of old!
With cunning suddenness
I push the window out
And as quickly shut it again;
The fly still on the glass
But on the outside now.
Unmoving, sulking, it stays,
Its diamond eyes upon
Sugar and cake and him
Who plays dirty tricks on flies.

Roy Fuller

The poetry of earth is never dead:
   When all the birds are faint with the hot sun,
   And hide in cooling trees, a voice will run
From hedge to hedge about the new-mown mead;
That is the Grasshopper's – he takes the lead
   In Summer luxury, – he has never done
   With his delights; for when tired out with fun
He rests at ease beneath some pleasant weed.
The poetry of earth is ceasing never:
On a lone winter evening, when the frost
   Has wrought a silence, from the stove there shrills
The Cricket's song, in warmth increasing ever,
And seems to one in drowsiness half lost,
   The Grasshopper's among some grassy hills.

John Keats

Parting the meadow grasses
you may find him –
green as a mint
and delicate as hair,

So light
that the blade humps
under his body
quivering, weightless, there;

And so he makes
his high, particular music
thrumming
In the deep heart of summer. Then

Leaps
in a little silence
onto other
grasses; and starts again.

Jean Kenward

Through my lens, this greenfly on a rose-leaf
Becomes in an eye-wink a terrifying monster
Crouching upon the dark-green leathery surface:
Beside him shines a bright round bubble of dew.
How odd, how fearful the world must look to him
As he stares through HIS lens! He sees my face
(Forehead and curving nose and one huge eye
Looming down coldly at him, prying and peering);
My cat, green-tiger-striped with shadows; and that lizard,
A sliding pterodactyl, as it passes
Through the tall, tangled forest of the grasses.

                                        Clive Sansom

what I was I cannot remember
only darkness
and bright light
and the wriggle of my long white body
wrapped
in a silky dream
something within me
grows
something new
something yet to be
I change
and the world changes with me
I move
to the sound of a distant tune
my song has words
that only I can hear
soon so soon
I shall throw off this skin
and pull myself free from the old world
into the new

Robert Fisher

And other eyes than ours
Were made to look on flowers,
Eyes of small birds and insects small:
The deep sun-blushing rose
Round which the prickles close
Opens her bosom to them all.
The tiniest living thing
That soars on feathered wing,
Or crawls among the long grass out of sight
Has just as good a right
To its appointed portion of delight
As any King.

Christina Rossetti

Hurt No Living Thing

Hurt no living thing,
Ladybird nor butterfly,
Nor moth with dusty wing,
Nor cricket chirping cheerily,
Nor grasshopper, so light of leap,
Nor dancing gnat,
Nor beetle fat,
Nor harmless worms that creep.

Christina Rossetti

Ladybird! Ladybird! Fly away home,
Night is approaching, and sunset is come:
The herons are flown to their trees by the Hall;
Felt, but unseen, the damp dewdrops fall.
This is the close of a still summer day;
Ladybird! Ladybird! haste! fly away!

Emily Brontë

Ladybird

Tiniest of turtles!
Your shining back
Is a shell of orange
With spots of black.

How trustingly you walk
Across this land
Of hairgrass and hollows
That is my hand.

Your small wire legs,
So frail, so thin,
Their touch is swansdown
Upon my skin.

There! break out
Your wings and fly:
No tenderer creature
Beneath the sky.

Clive Sansom

In the cowslip pips I lie,
Hidden from the buzzing fly,
While green grass beneath me lies,
Pearled with dew like fishes' eyes,
Here I lie, a clock-a-clay,
Waiting for the time of day.

While grassy forest quakes surprise,
And the wild wind sobs and sighs,
My gold home rocks as like to fall,
On its pillar green and tall;
When the pattering rain drives by
Clock-a-clay keeps warm and dry.

Day by day and night by night,
All the week I hide from sight;
In the cowslip pips I lie,
In rain and dew, still warm and dry;
Day and night and night and day,
Red, black-spotted clock-a-clay.

My home shakes in wind and showers,
Pale green pillar topped with flowers,
Bending at the wild wind's breath,
Till I touch the grass beneath;
Here I live, lone clock-a-clay,
Watching for the time of day.

                                        John Clare

What is a locust?
Its head a grain of corn; its neck the hinge of a knife;
Its horns a bit of thread; its chest is smooth and burnished;
Its body is like a knife handle;
Its hock a saw; its spittle, ink;
Its underwings, clothing for the dead.
On the ground – it is laying eggs;
In flight – it is like the clouds.
Approaching the ground, it is rain glittering in the sun;
Lighting on a plant, it becomes a pair of scissors;
Walking, it becomes a razor;
Desolation walks with it.

Traditional, Malagasy

in the apple
is the maggot
sweet green apple
sang the maggot
wrap me in your milk-white arms
let me suck you
eat you love you
sang the maggot
in the apple
tunnel to the sugar
maggot nibble nibble
eat your fill
until your belly bursts with apple
tasting sweetness
oh the maggot
in the apple
tingles with a true love's longing
for the cider-tasting sweetness
in the apple
hanging rotten
on the tree grown
in the garden
in the apple
sweet green apple
sang the maggot

Robert Fisher

A swarm of flies . . . . . .
. . . .
. . . l e . . . . u . . . .
. . . f . w . . o . . n . . .
. . . . . . r . . . . d .
. . . .
. my head . . . .
. . . . today .
. I tried to . . . .
. . . . . . s . . . .
. . . . w . . . . .
. . . . a . . . .
. . . . t . . .
. . . . them .
. but they flew . . . .
. . . . .away

Robert Fisher

The Mosquito Knows

The mosquito knows full well, small as he is
he's a beast of prey.
But after all
he only takes his bellyful,
he doesn't put any blood in the bank.

D. H. Lawrence

i was talking to a moth
the other evening
he was trying to break into
an electric light bulb
and fry himself on the wires

why do you fellows
pull this stunt i asked him
because it is the conventional
thing for moths or why
if that had been an uncovered
candle instead of an electric
light bulb you would
now be a small unsightly cinder
have you no sense

plenty of it he answered
but at times we get tired
of using it
we get bored with the routine
and crave beauty
and excitement
fire is beautiful
and we know that if we get
too close it will kill us

but what does that matter
it is better to be happy
for a moment
and be burned up with beauty
than to live a long time
and be bored all the while

so we wad all our life up
into one little roll
and then we shoot the roll
that is what life is for
it is better to be a part of beauty
for one instant and then cease to
exist than to exist forever
and never be a part of beauty
our attitude toward life
is come easy go easy

we are like human beings
used to be before they became
too civilized to enjoy themselves

and before i could argue him
out of his philosophy
he went and immolated himself
on a patent cigar lighter
i do not agree with him
myself i would rather have
half the happiness and twice
the longevity

but at the same time i wish
there was something i wanted
as badly as he wanted to fry himself

archy (Don Marquis)

The Scorpion is as black as soot,
He dearly loves to bite;
He is a most unpleasant brute
To find in bed at night.

Hilaire Belloc

Stalks, lovely stalks.

Through succulent slime
Pierce petals, and leaves
As large as elephant ears.

A non-discriminating tongue.

Shoots, lovely shoots.

Humping along the damp,
Tanking-out luminous trails,
That my eye
Sips in the sun.

There cruised the thug of the underworld.

Rona M. Campbell

Shloup shlugal shlobsh shlip
Sligoosh skigoosh shligalop
Shiligigoloshlob skibablosh
Bleshoposlopsh

Puff! Pant! Nearly at the end of the cabbage leaf
Ah, time for another shlogoly bit of cabbage
Shlibylishious,
Oh no, here comes that stupid gardener again!
He must think I'm really stupid
If he thinks I'll eat those disgusting pellets,
Oh no, my sticky shlogy gunge isn't sticky enough
I'm falling,
It's all right I've landed in the long grass,
It'll take another week to get up on that leaf again
But I'm not in a hurry.

Jim Bremner, aged twelve

To grass, or leaf, or fruit, or wall
The snail sticks fast, nor fears to fall,
As if he grew there, house and all,
                            together.

Within that house secure he hides
When danger imminent betides,
Or storms, or other human harms besides
                            of weather.

Give but his horns the slightest touch,
His self-collecting power is such,
He shrinks into his house with much
                            displeasure.

Where'er he dwells, he dwells alone,
Except himself, has chattels none,
Well satisfied to be his own
                            whole treasure.

Thus, hermit-like, his life he leads,
Nor partner of his banquet needs,
And if he meets one, only feeds
                            the faster.

Who seeks him must be worse than blind,
(He and his house are so combined)
If finding it he fails to find
                            its master.

                        William Cowper

Or as the snail, whose tender horns being hit,
Shrinks backward in his shelly cave with pain,
And there, all smother'd up in shade doth sit,
Long after fearing to creep forth again . . .

William Shakespeare

The snail pushes through a green
night, for the grass is heavy
with water and meets over
the bright path he makes, where rain
has darkened the earth's dark. He
moves in a wood of desire,

pale antlers barely stirring
as he hunts. I cannot tell
what power is at work, drenched there
with purpose, knowing nothing.
What is a snail's fury? All
I think is that if later

I parted the blades above
the tunnel and saw the thin
trail of broken white across
litter, I would never have
imagined the slow passion
to that deliberate progress.

Thom Gunn

Along the playground tarmac
Signing it with his trail
Glides Hannibal the Hero
Hannibal the snail.

Under the burning sun
In the asphalt desert dust
Hannibal with a placard
'To the football field or bust!'

Spurning food or drink
Refusing offers of aid
Hannibal hurries slowly on
And won't be put in the shade.

His trail is snail miles long
Its silver is tarnished and dimming
But Hannibal shoulders his dusty shell
And points his horns to winning.

Triumphant he glides to the balm of the grass
Into the cool of the clover.
Hannibal's crossed his desert.
His impossible journey is over.

He slides through the dandelions
Exploring each stalk and stem byway
And could that be Hannibal singing
'I did it my way'?

Julie Holder

The mud-snail
crawls a little way
and the day is over

Gomei

The Spider

I'm told that the spider
Has coiled up inside her
Enough silky material
To spin an aerial
One-way track
To the moon and back
Whilst I
Cannot even catch a fly.

Anonymous

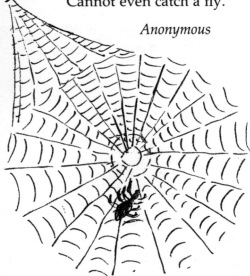

Hanging on a thread, like a wobbly tooth,
Gathering his pipe-cleaner legs to his body,
His pebble-like body shining in the sun,
Creeping like a miniature crab,
Spurts of speed, like bursts of conversation,
Darting to and fro,
Like a yo-yo up and down,
A puppet on a string.

The web glistening like the star of Bethlehem,
A tea-time doily,
A summer bonnet with fly-beads,
Springing trampoline, that can be raked down with a hand.
A decorated window,
Magnified, snow-flake falling down,
A fine kind of macramé,
The spider's larder.

Susan Garrett, aged ten

I have fought a grizzly bear,
Tracked a cobra to its lair,
Killed a crocodile who dared to cross my path;
But the thing I really dread
When I've just got out of bed
Is to find that there's a spider in the bath.

I've no fear of wasps or bees,
Mosquitoes only tease,
I rather like a cricket on the hearth;
But my blood runs cold to meet
In pyjamas and bare feet
With a great big hairy spider in the bath.

I have faced a charging bull in Barcelona,
I have dragged a mountain lioness from her cub,
I've restored a mad gorilla to its owner
But I don't dare to face that Tub . . .

What a frightful-looking beast –
Half an inch across at least –
It would frighten even Superman or Garth.
There's contempt it can't disguise
In the little beady eyes
Of the spider sitting glowering in the bath.

56] It ignores my every lunge
     With the back-brush and the sponge;
     I have bombed it with 'A Present from Penarth';
     But it doesn't mind at all –
     It just rolls into a ball
     And simply goes on squatting in the bath . . .

     For hours we have been locked in endless struggle;
     I have lured it to the deep end, by the drain;
     At last I think I've washed it down the plug-'ole
     But here it comes a-crawling up the chain!

     Now it's time for me to shave
     Though my nerves will not behave,
     And there's bound to be a fearful aftermath;
     So before I cut my throat
     I shall leave this final note:
     DRIVEN TO IT – BY THE SPIDER IN THE BATH!

          Michael Flanders and Donald Swann

The spider's touch, how exquisitely fine!
Feels at each thread, and lives along the line –

Alexander Pope

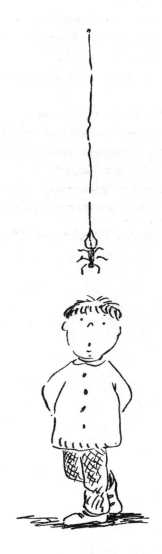

Knock, knock!
Who's there?
cried the spider.
Stand and wait!
But she knew by the
gentle tweak of the web
it was her mate.

Knock, knock!
Who's there?
cried the spider.
Call your name!
But she knew by the
soft tap-tap on the silk
her spiderlings came.

Knock, knock!
Who's there?
cried the spider.
Who goes by?
But she knew by the
shaking of her net
it was the fly.

                    Judith Nicholls

The family of stick insects grows larger
Their forest of privet grows green
The baby clings on to his mother's back
Camouflaged together with the rough stems and the
    soft leaves.

But the privet dries and dies
The stick insects' lives edge away
From soft green into stiffness
Does it feel strange, like getting arthritis?
Are they in terror of gnarling into bark itself,
Their life green draining into the sticks, and
    disappearing.

Now they are the harsh rough stems
Instead of new fresh leaves.
They are growing old.

                    Hannah Dawson, aged ten

Head with a tail,
Each day plumper,
On the way
From jelly to jumper.

Eric Finney

Answer: Tadpole

When the ripe pears droop heavily,
The yellow wasp hums loud and long
His hot and drowsy summer song.
A yellow flame he seems to be,
When darting suddenly from high
He lights where fallen peaches lie.

Yellow and black – this tiny thing's
A tiger soul on elfin wings.

William Sharp

Chase me, follow me round the room, knock over
Chairs and tables, bruise knees, spill books. High
I am then. If you climb up to me I go
Down. I have ways of detecting your least
Movements. I have radar you did not
Invent. You are afraid of me. I can
Sting hard. Ah but watch me bask in
The, to you, unbearable sun. I sport with it, am
Its jester and also its herald. Fetch a
Fly whisk. I scorn such. You must invent stings
For yourselves or else leave me alone, small, flying,
Buzzing tiger who have made a jungle out of the room
You thought safe,
Secure from all hurts and prying.

Elizabeth Jennings

Out on some nature ramble with the school
I found a hole in the ground tangled with grass
And kicked it – kicked it over again to feel
The earth all round my foot. It was a wasps' nest.
They rose in droning clouds, my head was wasps,
Hands in front of my eyes I stumbled down
The hill, myself a frantic hill of wasps –
One, cleaving to my temple, drilled right in.

My cries, they told me, could have been heard for miles,
But no one came. My fellow-pupils knew
Too well what lumps came up from red-hot weals,
And teachers felt they weren't paid to rescue
Boys from self-inflicted wounds. I ran
Blindly of course, crashed down into the wood,
Splashed across the beck, then up stream bellowing,
Shaking wasps off like confetti as I went.

The last one still to my temple clung, and stung
Again and again, digging in his hot lance.
I took him gently between my finger and thumb
And cast him against the air. He circled once
Glancing into the sun, then zoomed away.
There may be a moral here, though not for me;
But that is why, I think, I dream in this way,
Recalling things that nobody else would see.

Philip Hobsbaum

An effortless glider,
Defier of frictions
And gravity,
You skate on the pond's skin.
Your reflection
Your continual dancing partner.
The ease of your living
Cheers us.

John Cotton

Armoured dinosaur,
blundering through jungle grass by
dandelion-light.

Knight's headpiece, steel-hinged
orange-segment, ball-bearing,
armadillo-drop.

Pale peppercorn, pearled
eyeball; sentence without end,
my rolling full-stop.

Judith Nicholls

A woodworm I,
I lie entombed
In this dark case.
I feel the gloom;
I fear the feel
Of this dark room.
Body of death
I cry for life,
Never the grave
Has cried, 'Enough!'
Blind as I am
I crave for sight.
I bite my way
Towards the light.
I thank the Lord
For bread so rude,
And eat my coffin
For my food.

Alison Salkeld

Nobody loves me, everybody hates me
I'm going in the garden to eat worms.
Long slim slimy ones,
Short fat fuzzy ones,
Gooey-ooey-ooey ones.
The long slim slimy ones slip down easily,
The short fat fuzzy ones stick to your teeth,
And make you go urr urr yum yum!

Anonymous

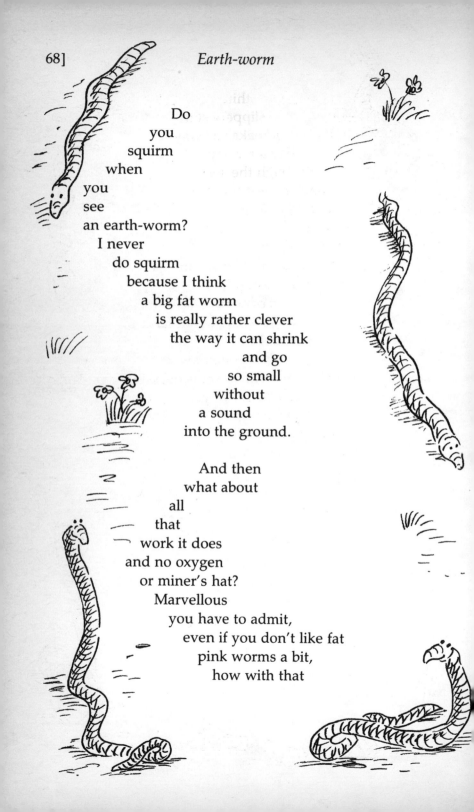

Do
you
squirm
when
you
see
an earth-worm?
I never
do squirm
because I think
a big fat worm
is really rather clever
the way it can shrink
and go
so small
without
a sound
into the ground.

And then
what about
all
that
work it does
and no oxygen
or miner's hat?
Marvellous
you have to admit,
even if you don't like fat
pink worms a bit,
how with that

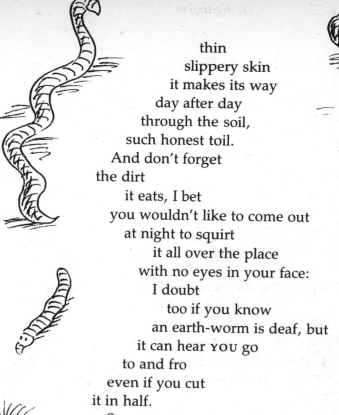

thin
slippery skin
it makes its way
day after day
through the soil,
such honest toil.
And don't forget
the dirt
it eats, I bet
you wouldn't like to come out
at night to squirt
it all over the place
with no eyes in your face:
I doubt
too if you know
an earth-worm is deaf, but
it can hear YOU go
to and fro
even if you cut
it in half.
So
do not laugh
or squirm
again
when
you
suddenly
see
a worm.

Leonard Clark

Long after humankind has gone
and cities lie empty
and the sound of machines
is stopped
in dark holes
there will be life
lying in cracks in the burnt earth
the white seeds of eggs
through the blowing dust come
scuttling legs

of animal life
they were the first
in some form they will be
the last of things
long after human hopes are lost
when the green world dies
once more life will rise
on tiny wings

Robert Fisher

The editor is grateful for permission to use the following copyright material:

'Ant' by Zoe Bailey, by permission of the author.

'Bee' by George Barker, from *The Alphabetical Zoo*, published by Faber and Faber Ltd.

'The Scorpion' by Hilaire Belloc, from *Cautionary Verses by Hilaire Belloc*, published by Gerald Duckworth Ltd.

'Slug' by Jim Bremner, from *Cadbury's Seventh Book of Children's Poetry*, copyright © Cadbury Ltd.

'Simply a Slug' by Rona M. Campbell, by permission of the author.

'Earthworm' and 'Three Butterflies' by Leonard Clark, by permission of Robert A. Clark.

'Water Boatman' by John Cotton, by permission of the author.

'Stick Insect Growing Old' by Hannah Dawson, from *Cadbury's Eighth Book of Children's Poetry*, copyright © Cadbury Ltd.

'The Fly' by Walter de la Mare, by permission of the Literary Trustees of Walter de la Mare and the Society of Authors as their representative.

'A Dragonfly' by Eleanor Farjeon, from *Silver, Sand and Snow*, published by Michael Joseph Ltd., by permission of David Higham Associates Ltd.

'Earwig O' and 'Riddle' by Eric Finney, by permission of the author.

'The Spider' by Michael Flanders, from *The Songs of Michael Flanders and Donald Swann*, by permission of Mrs Claudia Flanders.

'The Cricket' by John Fuller, by permission of the author.

'Spiders' by Susan Garrett, from *Cadbury's First Book of Children's Poetry*, copyright © Cadbury Ltd.

'The Centipede' from *Beast's Choir* by Carmen Bernos de Gatzold, translated by Rumer Godden, published by Macmillan.

'Flying Crooked' by Robert Graves, from *Collected Poems* by Robert Graves, by permission of A. P. Watt Ltd.

'Considering the Snail' by Thom Gunn, from *My Sad Captains*, published by Faber and Faber Ltd.

'Xestobium Nifovillosum' and 'Xylocorus Galactinus' by Michael Harrison, by permission of the author.

'A Country Matter' by Philip Hobsbaum, by permission of the author.

72] 'Grasshopper' by Jean Kenward, by permission of the author.
'Cabbage White Butterfly' and 'Wasp in a Room' by Elizabeth Jennings, by permission of David Higham Associates.
'The Whole Truth and Nothing' by Ian Larmont, by permission of the author.
'Woodlouse' by Judith Nicholls, from *Midnight Forest* by Judith Nicholls and 'Who's there?' by Judith Nicholls, from *Midnight Forest* by Judith Nicholls, published by Faber and Faber Ltd.
'Lament of the Woodworm in the Piano' by Alison Salkeld, by permission of the author.
'Ladybirds' by Clive Sansom, from *The Golden Unicorn*, and 'Magic' by Clive Sansom, from *A Song of Sunlight*, by permission of David Higham Associates.
'The Tickle Rhyme' by Ian Seraillier, by permission of the author.

Acknowledgements are also made to the few copyright holders whom the editor has been unable to trace in spite of careful enquiry.